A STINKY HISTORY OF
TOILETS

NEON SQUID

CONTENTS

WHAT DO WE DO WITH ALL THIS POOP?

This is a question humans have been asking themselves since the very beginning. In this book we'll explore all the clever solutions people have tried over the past 300,000 years. But just how much poop are we talking about?

WHAT A LOAD OF POOP!

ONE ADULT POOPS...

Most adults poop about once a day, and it usually weighs about 15 oz (420 g). Add that up, and an adult's poop weighs about the same as:

25 APPLES PER WEEK

ALL HUMANS POOP...

There are eight billion people living on Earth. So if we add it all up, together our poop weighs about the same as:

70 EMPIRE STATE BUILDINGS PER WEEK

200 PYRAMIDS PER YEAR

ONE PANDA
PER YEAR

READY, SET, POOP!

Scientists have found that it takes us about 12 seconds to do a poop. The same is true for many animal species, regardless of their size!

`00:00:12`

WHAT MAKES POOP, POOP?

Poop is 75% water. The rest is undigested food and mucus from our intestines.

WHY IS IT BROWN?

Your liver makes an orange slime called bile to help digest food. Mix it in with what you've eaten and it all turns brown.

WHY IS IT STINKY?

Farting bacteria! These teeny creatures in your gut feast on the food you ate and release gases.

PARP!!!

PARDON YOU!

5

PICK YOUR SPOT!

Throughout history, many cultures didn't have special places for people to go to the toilet—they just expected everyone to avoid creating a "poop pile-up" in any one spot. This method worked pretty well when people weren't too crowded together, but not everyone liked the idea. There isn't a right or wrong answer to where people should pee and poop— everyone does things differently!

THE STONE AGE

Millions of years ago, humans probably just pooped behind any bush. Archaeologists haven't found any signs that they used specific spots as "poop zones."

MUST FOLLOW THE LAW!

Soldiers in ancient Israel followed very strict Jewish laws when it came to pooping. They had to find a random spot outside camp, dig a hole before they did their business (even if they were desperate!), then bury their poop.

DIFFERENCE OF OPINION

When Portuguese colonisers arrived in the African country of Angola they were annoyed that the locals refused to use their European-style latrines. Meanwhile, the Angolans were baffled that the newcomers didn't understand how rude (and *super gross!*) it was to poop in the same place as someone else.

UGH! THESE PEOPLE JUST DON'T GET IT!

FREE FOR ALL

Pooping near your house or in your neighbor's field was a big no-no for the Wai-Wai people of Guyana in South America. Instead, families left strips of shared land between farms—this way everyone in the neighborhood could always find a fresh spot to poop.

KEEP MOVING

The Tatar people of North Asia moved around a lot and hated the idea of pooping in the same place. "I hope you stay in one place so long, you have to smell your own poop!" was one of their nastiest curses.

FANCY SEEING YOU HERE!

Lucky for us, dung beetles clean up poop by eating it!

SWIMMING IN SEWAGE

In many places around the world, a popular solution to human waste disposal is to dump everything in nearby oceans, lakes, or rivers. However, when that same water is also used to provide drinking water, it becomes a problem. Bacteria or parasites (tiny creatures that can live inside animals or people) from human waste can spread dangerous diseases.

SMELLBOURNE, AUSTRALIA

Gold was discovered in parts of Australia in 1851. This brought half a million immigrants to the country in one year, so things got gross, fast. Without sewers, the streets of Melbourne—and the Yarra river— were absolutely full of sewage. The stench got so bad, newspapers playfully renamed the city "Smellbourne."

POOP OVERBOARD!

Cruise ships pour over a billion liters of sewage into the ocean every year. Most make the sewage safe before they dump it, but some still don't.

FISH FEEDERS

Hanging latrines are toilets built over a body of water, where the waste falls directly underneath. Sometimes they're set up over fishponds so the poop falls down and feeds the fish!

HUMANS SHOULD NEVER DRINK CONTAMINATED WATER.

Privies are probably the most popular toilet in history.

ENGAGED

GOOD THING THIS IS SO FAR FROM THE HOUSE!

PRIVIES

How about digging a pit for our poop? Families across the world have done this for thousands of years. Plop a seat on top and you've got a privy. Privies can be stinky, quite dark, and freezing in the winter. Once one is full, the family seals it up and digs another.

PUMPING POOP

In the past, people dug privies near wells, not knowing that sewage was seeping into the soil. So the stuff that left their body in the privy . . . they ended up drinking it again.

FIFTH IN LINE! NOT TOO COLD, NOT TOO STINKY. RESULT!

Some families tied a rope from their house to their privy so they could "go" during the night. In 1910, one English family with 11 children would all go out together.

The family had three seats in their privy: small, medium, and large. They always matched their butt size to the hole.

But that didn't always stop them from falling in!

VIKING MIDDENS
& A HISTORIC POOP

When Vikings lived in Jorvik (present day York, UK) they threw everything they didn't want into one nasty pile known as a midden. When archaeologists stumbled upon it 1,000 years later, it was still stinky! They knew it would tell them a lot about the past.

SUCH A DUMP

The Jorvik midden was next to a river called the Ouse. Before all the rubbish decayed, wet soil "mummified" and preserved it instead! Here are some of the things that got buried.

Ivory board game

Padlock and key

1,700 leather shoes

Antler comb

Silver coins

Amber jewelry

42 horse bone ice skates

250,000 pieces of pottery

Rare sock

POOP . . . OR TREASURE?

The midden contained the biggest fossilized human poop ever discovered. It revealed that Vikings' bodies were infested with thousands of itchy parasites, including worms that wriggle out of your nose and eyes!

"AS PRECIOUS AS THE CROWN JEWELS!" —BONE JONES, ARCHAEOLOGIST

DIGGING IT UP

When archaeologists dug up the Jorvik midden, the smell was horrendous! But they kept on digging because the things they found were amazing: 40,000 mummified objects!

DID SOMEONE FART?

USE IT AGAINST YOUR ENEMIES

One way to deal with all the poop you're creating is to put it to work . . . against your enemies! Whether it's offensive (catapulting poop) or defensive (hiding treasure under a privy), this sticky sludge makes for a *very* powerful weapon.

BIOLOGICAL WARFARE

As the Black Death plague swept the world in the 1300s, Mongol armies mixed gunpowder with poop from their own infected soldiers, lit it on fire, then catapulted it over enemy walls! The exploding poop balls infected everyone inside.

ERASMUS THE (ALMOST) INVINCIBLE

A Slovenian legend about a knight named Erasmus says that an army attacked his castle for a *whole year* but still couldn't destroy it!

So his enemies bribed a servant to betray him.

The next time Erasmus visited the garderobe . . .

DON'T FLOAT IN THE MOAT

Castle residents used garderobes—outhouses hanging off the castle wall—so everybody's poop landed right in the moat! No wonder attacking soldiers refused to swim across them—castle moats were more sewer than swimming pool.

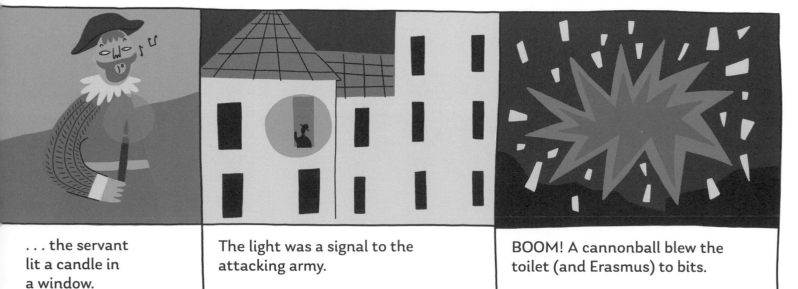

. . . the servant lit a candle in a window.

The light was a signal to the attacking army.

BOOM! A cannonball blew the toilet (and Erasmus) to bits.

POOP PARTIES

ANCIENT ROME

Two thousand years ago, the Romans built some fancy public toilets. You could sit and chat with the whole town in a 60-seater toilet! Running water underneath swished poop and pee into a nearby river or ocean. It seemed like the perfect toilet, but sea creatures knew how to swim upstream . . .

Historians found ancient graffiti on the walls, such as "Cacator cave malum" ("Pooper beware").

CACATOR CAVE MALUM!

Scented candles masked the smell.

OKAY, ALL DONE. NOW YOU CAN USE THIS SPONGE!

There are stories of sea snakes biting people's butts through the toilets, and once even an octopus emerged!

Before using shared sea sponges to wipe their butts, Romans would stick the sponges in the little trough of water by their toes to "clean" them.

Does pooping have to be a solitary thing? Most of us spend more than 90 minutes each week on the toilet. That adds up to about 256 days of our lives! As a result, some cultures decided that toilet time was better spent together.

THE WILD WEST

Cowboys built all kinds of group toilets. North Americans named them for how many seats they had (two-holer, three-holer, four-holer), Australians called them dunnies, and South American gauchos called them *letrinas*.

Tall sunflowers were planted around the toilets for privacy, so when cowboys had to go, they'd just look around for sunflowers.

The wooden seats were warm, but imagine the splinters!

Wise cowboys took sticks with them to sweep for venomous snakes and spiders.

A corn on the cob was the wiping implement of choice.

CLEANING UP THE MESS

"It's easy to get rid of pee and poop, just toss it out of the window!" That's what most Europeans would have said 1,000 years ago. But just picture the streets! They were even more stinky than you can imagine . . . and someone always had to clean them up.

GONGFERMORS

What if you were allowed to stay up all night . . . but you had to shovel buckets of poop? Gongfermors cleaned the streets and were forced to work at night.

FROZEN POOP

Today, people in the Siberian tundra, in the north of Russia, have a clever way of cleaning their cesspits (poop-filled holes in the ground): wait for them to freeze! The icy blocks are hacked to pieces with a pickaxe and hauled away. No stink, no slime, no mess.

Back then, high heels weren't for fashion, they were for walking above the muck.

See your enemy passing by? Time to empty the pot!

WATCH OUT!

UNTOUCHABLES

For thousands of years, India operated a "caste system," where you did different jobs depending on which caste you were in. People called Dalits ("untouchables") did all the filthy jobs. Despite new laws, this still happens in some places.

Women had to carry household waste away with a woven basket.

Men were made to do the more dangerous job of cleaning cesspits.

THE STORY OF CHOLERA

During the 1800s, millions of people crowded into the world's biggest and dirtiest cities—and a terrifying disease called cholera began killing them. Cholera spreads when infected poop gets into our water or food. Overflowing cesspits, filthy markets, and rivers full of sewage caused thousands of deaths every year.

BAD BACTERIA

The cholera bacteria, *vibrio cholerae*, attacks the body through the digestive system. It causes dehydration from diarrhea.

British Jamaican nurse Mary Seacole treated cholera patients all over the world.

Blood-sucking leeches

TRIAL AND ERROR

European doctors used treatments that did more harm than good, including leeches that sucked out a patient's "bad blood." Asian and Caribbean doctors gave patients herbal teas or other medicinal drinks, which probably didn't help—but at least they didn't make things worse!

SOLVING THE MYSTERY

Back in the 19th century, doctors didn't know about bacteria yet and thought bad smells caused the disease. But London doctor John Snow suspected the problem was dirty water. The trouble was, nobody would listen! After years of mapping cholera outbreaks, John finally convinced the city to remove an infected public water pump—and people stopped dying!

YOU KNOW NOTHING, JOHN SNOW!

Japanese monks built a hundred-person toilet in the 1300s to collect poop for fertilizer.

DON'T LET IT GO TO WASTE

Why let all that precious poop and prized pee go to waste?! Whether for cleaning clothes, growing crops, or starting fires, creative humans all over the world have dreamed up amazing ways to reuse their waste!

POOP FUEL

In many places around the world, poop is dried into bricks or flakes, which can be used as fertilizer or fuel.

PLANTS LOVE POOP

Poop can make a great fertilizer, because it recycles useful nutrients and minerals back into the soil, which helps plants to grow more strongly. However, it needs to be properly dried first or infectious bacteria, parasites, and all kinds of other icky stuff could end up contaminating the crops.

Pee is full of useful minerals, so it makes great fertilizer too!

PEE WASH

In ancient Rome, laundries placed huge clay pots on the street for passersby to pee in. They used the pee to clean clothes—the ammonia in the urine helped keep togas sparkling white.

Some enemies claimed that Romans used pee as mouthwash, but they probably didn't.

DON'T TRY THIS AT HOME!

A ROYAL FLUSH

Have you ever thought of your poops as wonderful, precious things? Kings and queens across the world wanted everyone to believe that their poops were as magnificent as they were. Naturally, those special poops called for special toilets—simple privies and shared rooms wouldn't do. Instead, royals did their business in very posh containers called "close stools."

THE WORST JOB IN THE WORLD?

One of the top jobs in all of England used to be the Groom of the Stool. You watched Queen Elizabeth I poop into her fancy close stool, then handed her a cloth to wipe. It was your job to clean up afterward too!

LOUIS XIV

People from all over the world wanted to meet King Louis of France. But when they did, he just sat on his throne . . . Turns out it was actually a toilet, and he spent the whole day pooping!

THE JAPANESE TALE OF THE SHOGUN'S STOOL

This folk story was told to show how much people used to honor shoguns—Japanese warrior kings. Do you think it's true?

Two hundred years ago, a powerful shogun was hunting with his friends in a forest.

"It's that special time, everyone!" he said. But his friends had forgotten his close stool.

He rushed to a nearby village, but those lowly peasants only had privies!

Instead, the shogun walked into the best house in the village hoping for a miracle.

He pulled down his pants and pooped right in the middle of the floor, then left!

Everyone in the village honored the poop forever after!

TRAP THE SMELL

Nobody likes the stinky smell of poop. But how can we avoid it? Over thousands of years, we've used these basic ways to trap the smell: burying it with dirt in a box, covering it with water, or keeping something else nearby that has a stronger (and nicer) smell. Which method do you use at your house?

"YOU DARE INSULT ME, SIR?!"

THE AJAX

If your toilet uses water to trap the smell, you can thank Sir John Harrington. He invented the Ajax 450 years ago for Queen Elizabeth I. He wrote a book about it, but it was so rude and gross that the queen banished him! Sir John named the toilet after the mythical sea captain Ajax. Anyone who insulted the captain, he said, would be struck down with diarrhea!

Turn a crank, and water from the top cistern washed poop into the bottom. It was the first flushing toilet!

MAYA OVEN-TOILET

Historically, the Maya of Central America cleverly reused cooking pits as toilets. First, cook. Second, eat. Third, poop! Last, pour the quicklime water you used to cook into the pit. The strong chemical traps the smell completely.

Quicklime is a powerful chemical made by burning limestone.

STEP ASIDE, KITTY

Earth closets were very common in prisons and schools. They were basically cat litter for humans. After someone pooped, a layer of dirt would cover up the waste, trapping the horrible smell.

THAT'S MY LITTER!

NANTEN TREE

In Japan, this tree smells so sweet and lovely that people call it heavenly bamboo. It was planted outside all privies to mask the smell. Hundreds of years later, it's still a common air freshener in Japanese bathrooms.

If you lived near the ocean centuries ago, you might have chosen seashells as your tool of choice.

Humans have always used leaves as toilet paper. Many still do. Just be sure to avoid the stinging nettles!

A BRIEF HISTORY OF TOILET PAPER

The ancient Greeks used round stones…

Toilet paper! It's hard to imagine a world without it, but people throughout history have used all kinds of things to clean up—from sponges to seashells. Once the world discovered convenient, easy-tear toilet rolls, bathrooms would never be the same.

…and broken pottery to scrape. Ouch!

Would you wipe your butt with a corn on the cob?

Wooden poop-scrapers were popular in Japan around 500 CE.

28

Magazines were recycled as toilet paper. They made for convenient bathroom reading material too!

Ancient poop found on Chinese "hygiene sticks" proves the Vikings weren't the only ones plagued by parasites!

CHINA vs USA

American Joseph Gayetty often gets credit for "inventing" toilet paper in the 1800s, but the Chinese had been using it for 1,200 years before Gayetty was even born! During the Ming Dynasty, China was getting through 100 million sheets every year.

KNOCK KNOCK!

WHO'S THERE?

THE INVENTORS OF TOILET PAPER!

WAIT, WHAT? I INVENTED TOILET PAPER LAST WEEK!

MY GREAT-GREAT-GREAT-GREAT-GREAT-GREAT-GREAT-GREAT-GREAT... GRANDFATHER WOULD LIKE A WORD ABOUT THAT, JOE!

LET'S BUILD SEWERS!

From digging huge tunnels to lifting whole towns, constructing sewers is a lot of work. But all across the world and throughout history, people have dreamed up amazing ways to keep their sewage out of sight—and off the streets.

MINOAN CRETE

On the Mediterranean island of Crete in ancient times, they had flushing toilets . . . sort of. A servant stationed outside the door would pour water into a trench that ran underneath the toilet. How fancy!

MOHENJO-DARO

Over 4,500 years ago, this ancient city (in modern Pakistan) had an amazing sewer system. Individual toilets were connected to street channels that carried the waste out of the city. Once those narrow channels filled up, people would just add more bricks to raise the height of the walls surrounding them!

ANCIENT ROME

The Cloaca Maxima ("Great Sewer") of ancient Rome was more like a massive underground river than a modern sewer. Huge tunnels channeled waste from public toilets and street drains out into the river Tiber. A few sections are still used today!

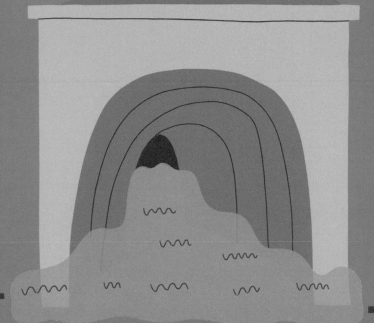

ANCIENT CHINA

Starting around 4,000 years ago, many Chinese cities began fitting cone-shaped clay tubes together to make strong, flexible sewer pipes.

DON'T DIG, LIFT!

In 1858, the city of Chicago, USA, faced a huge problem. They didn't have a sewer system.

As a result, the streets were covered in muck!

So the town used jackscrews to raise the buildings (with people inside!) and built new streets.

And the old streets below were turned into sewers!

GASSY EXPLOSIONS

When pipes were connected to sewers full of rotting poop, gases traveled up the pipes. When those gases met a candle flame inside the bathroom . . . BOOM! Exploding toilets.

DID YOU HEAR THAT?!

HOW EMBARRASSING!

If you didn't have an exploding toilet, you had a noisy toilet. For prudish Victorians, nothing was more horrifying than the neighbors knowing when they pooped!

PROBLEMS WITH PIPES

THE JENNINGS TEST

Inventor George Jennings created a super-toilet. In 1884 it managed to flush down ten apples, one large sponge, and four pieces of greasy paper—all at once!

HOLD YOUR NOSE

The sewers were full of sludge and goo and rats and poop. That awful smell crept out of every vent and manhole in town, and right up people's pipes.

Pipes make it easy for stuff to swoosh down, but everything that goes down can also come *up*! Romans didn't like pipes in their homes because sea creatures swam up into their living rooms. 1,800 years later, Victorians decided to try again, with smaller pipes. No more octopuses in the house, but the new problems were even worse . . .

S-BEND

Scottish inventor Alexander Cumming discovered that keeping water in the pipe by bending it meant that nasty sewer gases couldn't float back up.

I ALSO INVENTED A MUCH BETTER FLUSH!

YES, MY NAME IS CRAPPER. WHY DO YOU ASK?

U-BEND

Thomas Crapper improved Alexander's S-bend so it wouldn't clog or overflow. He also helped make flushing toilets popular in people's homes.

BUILDING THE BEST TOILET

John Harrington's Ajax toilet (see page 26) introduced the world to the flush, but it would be another 200 years before the technology really caught on. Once it did, the battle for the title of Best Toilet Inventor was on—and competition was fierce! Across the UK, new inventions were popping up everywhere.

COME AND SEE THE FUTURE OF POOPING!

SURELY NOBODY WILL EVER FORGET TO PUT THIS SEAT BACK DOWN.

REVEREND HENRY MOULE

Henry invented his earth closet to prevent cholera in poor neighborhoods. Users pulled a lever to release a layer of dirt that covered and dried out the poop, so the waste could be safely dumped outside later.

SOME FANCY FOLK LIKE MY TOILET BETTER BECAUSE IT'S SILENT!

THOMAS TWYFORD

Another Thomas made two big advances in toilet technology: a hinged seat that could be lifted up and down and an all-in-one-piece porcelain toilet that was much easier to clean.

GEORGE JENNINGS

George wanted everyone to love toilets like he did. His fancy public toilets at London's Great Exhibition in 1851 were wildly popular—over 800,000 visitors paid to use them.

I'LL NEVER POOP IN A HOLE IN THE GROUND AGAIN!

LET'S BURN IT

Burning poop *seems* like a good way to make it disappear, but it's actually very difficult. Poop is 75% water, and the rest is made up of a weird mixture of bits. This means it doesn't burn evenly, and it certainly doesn't smell good.

WWI LOO (PART I)

Army camps have conducted the biggest experiments in poop-burning. During World War I, soldiers had to camp in mud trenches for years. Their toilets were logs balanced over a giant sludgy pit. They poured oil on top to trap flies.

DON'T SPLASH! DON'T FALL IN!

A BOX OF POOP

Later in World War I, trying to improve on the open flaming pit, the American Army built huge excrement incinerators, or poop burners. They had layers inside where air dried out the wet poop. But it used way too much fuel and the smoke was terribly stinky.

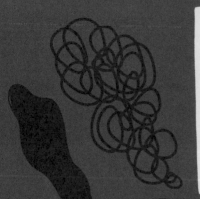

WWI LOO (PART II)

Every two days the sludgy pit had to be burned. The soldiers threw in straw and petrol, lit it on fire, then stirred the flaming poop stew with big sticks.

TOILETS ON FIRE!

Nowadays, scientists have found easier ways to burn poop. In Antarctica, explorers use incinerator toilets to avoid contaminating the habitat. They simply use the toilet, close the lid, and push a button! And just like magic—or should we say science—the poop turns to ashes.

A paper liner inside the toilet provides dry fuel.

When it's done, the ashes are packed up to be safely disposed.

SQUAT . . .

Squat toilets are common in Asia, Africa, and the Middle East. They only need a bit of water, so they're good for the planet. Plus, squatting squeezes your guts, which makes pooping easier!

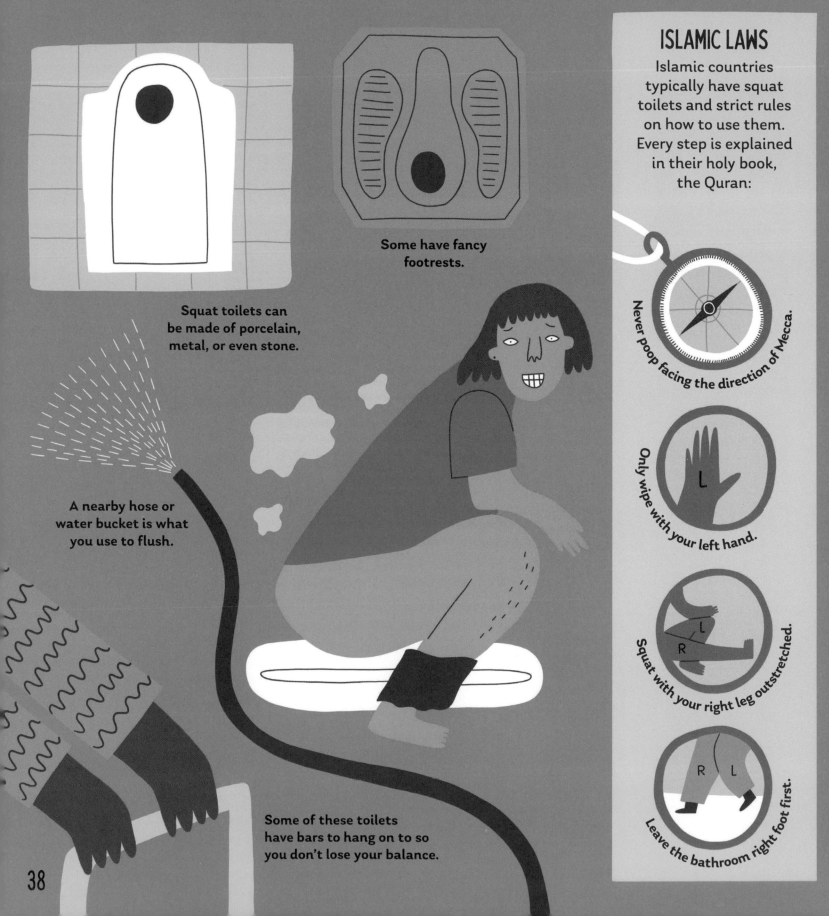

Squat toilets can be made of porcelain, metal, or even stone.

Some have fancy footrests.

A nearby hose or water bucket is what you use to flush.

Some of these toilets have bars to hang on to so you don't lose your balance.

ISLAMIC LAWS

Islamic countries typically have squat toilets and strict rules on how to use them. Every step is explained in their holy book, the Quran:

Never poop facing the direction of Mecca.

Only wipe with your left hand.

Squat with your right leg outstretched.

Leave the bathroom right foot first.

SIT . . .

If you live in Northern Europe or anywhere in the Americas, you probably have a sitting toilet. In Southern Europe, South America, and Japan, you might also have a bidet.

What is your toilet seat of choice?

A sitting toilet has a button, chain, or lever to flush it.

Bidets are like little bathtubs for your butt.

OR STAND?

In Europe and the Americas, you might pee standing up at a urinal, also called a *pissoir*. Urinals for women are just starting to catch on.

39

SO GOOD YOU CAN DRINK IT

1. After flushing the loo . . . what happens to your poop?

Flushing toilets are amazing inventions, but where exactly does that pee or poop go after it disappears down the drain? In about half of the world, it goes to a sewage treatment plant to be cleaned, processed, and turned into fresh water. Treatment plants come in different shapes and sizes, but the one that deals with your waste might look something like this . . .

2. Hidden pipes inside the walls of your home connect your toilet to big sewer pipes underneath your house.

4. Sewage passes through a huge metal screen that filters out any unusual objects—like footballs, mattresses, or even dead cows!

3. Those sewer pipes then connect to larger, then larger, then LARGER pipes that run under all the streets in your town. Eventually, they take everything you flushed down your toilet to the sewage treatment plant.

5. The sewage is then shaken and stirred in a big tank to make dirt and sand sink to the bottom, while poop stays floating near the top.

6. Some treatment plants use giant "balloon bags" to collect the gas from decaying poop so they can turn it into electricity!

PARP

Special bacteria get rid of the poop by eating it!

7. Oil and soap sometimes float at the top of the tanks, so special rakes are used to clean the water's surface.

8. Eventually the remaining water is so clean it's safe to drink! It can then be pumped into a nearby river, lake, or ocean.

TOILETS TODAY

BEHIND A BUSH

Are you one of the 494 million people who go in a different spot each time? Don't go near a water source, but try to go where dung beetles live! And make sure you wash your hands with soap afterward.

SHARED TOILETS

600 million people share group toilets. Make sure you have a hand-washing station nearby so no one spreads germs. Do NOT share butt-wiping sponges like the Romans did. Eeeww!

PRIVIES WITH NO PIPES

160 million people carry water to their homes from lakes or rivers, which might be close to privies. Always boil the water to kill any germs before using it.

Most of the historical toilets we've seen in this book are still used in different parts of the world today. Thanks to everything we've learned about toilets, we can make sure all of these ways of doing our business are safe by following some simple rules!

FLUSHING TOILETS

If your toilet looks something like this, check it has an S-bend so it doesn't explode! (Don't worry . . . it's required these days.) These toilets use a lot of water, so see if you can reduce the water use by checking for leaks or using a low-flow model. Water is far too precious to waste!

Some people play special noises and use fresh sprays to make pooping less embarrassing.

MOOOO!

the SOAPS
TONIGHT
THIS WEEK

HANGING LATRINES

If your latrine hangs over a river or if you dump your buckets into a river, it's time to move your spot away from the water. Although the fish may like it, it's terrible for the people nearby. It will take work, but your actions will be an act of kindness for the planet!

THE FUTURE OF POOP

What will the toilets of the future be like? The truth is, nobody knows for sure. When you look at all the amazing inventions people have dreamed up over the years—from Queen Elizabeth I's close stool to toilets in outer space—one thing is for sure: humans will keep coming up with amazing toilet innovations!

TOILETS IN SPACE

Astronauts have used all kinds of strange toilets—from simple tube-and-funnel systems that quite literally suck away the waste, to toilets you have to strap yourself into!

PEE POWER

When you don't have water pipes or electricity, a toilet that turns pee into power can feel like magic. One invention creates electricity with every flush. Other toilets can power lights for a building—or even a whole village!

NANO MEMBRANE TOILETS

This amazing invention doesn't need pipes, water, or power. A spinning toilet bowl separates poop from pee, turns the pee into clean water (which can be used to do the laundry), and burns the poop to create enough electricity to charge your phone!

SMART TOILETS

Smart toilets can recognize different butts and keep track of how long it takes for you to . . . *ahem* . . . relieve yourself. They can even tell what's inside each poop, which might help to diagnose diseases.

TIME

SMELL-O-METER

0 1 2 3 4 5 6 7 8 9 10

hard   soft

hot chocolate
bananas
prunes
juice
corn
beans
milk

2 wipes

POOPS THIS WEEK

4
3
2
1

M T W T F S S

GLOSSARY

ARCHAEOLOGIST

Someone who finds evidence of human history by digging up stuff we leave behind.

BIDET

A basin used for cleaning your private parts, like a little shower for your butt.

CASTE SYSTEM

A way of dividing society based on people's wealth, occupation, or race. This gives certain people a lot more power than others.

CASTLE MOAT

A pool of water that surrounds a castle to prevent enemies from attacking it.

CESSPIT

A hole in the ground where waste (usually poop and pee) is stored.

CLOSE STOOL

A portable toilet in a fancy box that was used by royals or very rich families.

DEHYDRATION

A dangerous health condition where your body isn't getting enough water.

DIARRHEA

Unstoppable runny poop caused by germs or bacteria.

GARDEROBE

A toilet in a castle, usually hung over the ground or above a moat.

GONGFERMOR

A medieval street-cleaner who shoveled up poop at night.

LATRINE

A temporary outdoor toilet.

PRIVY

A private toilet, usually in a small hut built over a pit.

SEWER

A large underground tunnel or pipe that carries waste and dirty water away.

TREATMENT PLANT

A place where human waste is treated and turned into clean water.

URINE

Another word for pee. Urine is mostly made up of water and salt.

INDEX

This has been a

NEON ⬛ SQUID

production

Katie: To Zack and Daisy, who could talk about poop all day long.

Olivia: To Matthew, who is always my most enthusiastic cheerleader! Even when it means getting excited about toilets with me every day for a year.

Authors: Olivia Meikle and Katie Nelson
Illustrator: Ella Kasperowicz

Editorial Assistant: Malu Rocha
US Editor: Jill Freshney
Proofreader: Georgina Coles
Special Consultant: Jennifer Meikle
Kid Editors: James Warby and Kade Warby

Copyright © 2024 St. Martin's Press
120 Broadway, New York, NY 10271

Created for St. Martin's Press
by Neon Squid
The Stables, 4 Crinan Street,
London, N1 9XW

EU representative: Macmillan
Publishers Ireland Ltd,
1st Floor, The Liffey Trust Centre,
117–126 Sheriff Street Upper,
Dublin 1, D01 YC43

10 9 8 7 6 5 4 3 2 1

Library of Congress Cataloging-in-Publication Data is available.

Printed and bound in Guangdong, China by Leo Paper Products Ltd.

ISBN: 978-1-684-49373-9

Published in March 2024.

www.neonsquidbooks.com